The JFK Assassination

A Technical Review of the Evidence

By Anthony Rante, P.E.

To my wife Mary

CONTENTS

Introduction	3
Chapter 1 – Overview	9
Chapter 2 – Prior Knowledge	22
Chapter 3 – Texas School Book Depository and Dealey Plaza	28
Chapter 4 – Bullet Wounds	34
Chapter 5 – The Zapruder Film	44
Chapter 6 – Aftermath in Dealey Plaza and Other Important Testimony	63
Chapter 7 – Additional Oswald Details	77
Epilogue	86
References	95

Introduction

About thirty years ago, I started reading about the JFK assassination. I had no beliefs on whether or not the assassination was a conspiracy, or was a single shooter with an agenda. Growing up, I had watched some of the news specials trying to make sense out of the massive confusion surrounding this event. Was it the mafia, was it the CIA, was it the Dallas police department, was it Cuba, was it Russia… or was it a single "lone nut" who decided on this action? I wanted to learn more. But as I tried, I quickly realized that there is so much information and so many points of view, that anyone reading about this topic needs to be careful about what to believe and what to disregard. The phrase "separating the wheat from chaff" probably best describes the proper approach for someone researching this event.

Once you begin to read and research this topic, the amount of information that this story includes becomes enormous. One thread of information expands to several new branches and you soon realize that the topic cannot be covered in a single text or study. For example, the assassination event took place in Dallas Texas, but there are branches that lead to New Orleans, Miami, Cuba, Russia, North Carolina, and

Chicago. The cast of characters that we have learned about in this story are vast with ties to the CIA, FBI, MAFIA, and other political factions. Unfortunately, once you start to research any of these areas you typically end with the main character mysteriously dying and the thread ends cold. One example of this is the story of Lee Bowers. Mr. Bowers was an employee for the railroad working close to where the assassination occurred. On the day of the event, he was stationed in the switching tower in close proximity to the event. He had witnessed several strange occurrences around the time of the assassination and he was one of the only witnesses in this area. He died a few years later in an auto accident on an empty road.

The year of the assassination is 1963. During that time, photograph and some film technology was available. Since this was a visit to Dallas by the president of the United States, naturally many people attended the parade. Several important photographs and video clips were taken that day. This evidence is available and does provide insight to what took place. As you will soon find out, a key film of the assassination was taken by Abraham Zapruder. Mr. Zapruder owned a business near Dealey Plaza. He joined the crowds to watch and film the motorcade. While filming the president's limousine, he captured a detailed record of the assassination.

In this text, specific information about the assassination is presented. I am only presenting information that I feel is the most critical and will give the reader an overview of what took place that day. When testimony and interviews are used, I tried to be sure they give the most pertinent information and the details are consistent over time. Testimony that is referenced in this text in general has stood the test of time. The originator has provided the same testimony and point of view over several decades.

As noted above, the many roads one can travel in this research is a tremendous undertaking. The many hours I have spent have helped me steer my focus on the most important aspects of this story. Wherever possible, my effort is to highlight facts that can support a completed and detailed review. In my personal ventures and activities, I always try to meet objectives and reach conclusions. The study of the JFK assassination is no different. The evidence we have in this case is not always detailed to the point we can reach an exact fact. Nevertheless, the opportunity to obtain a clearer understanding is there. We can follow scientific details like time and physics and couple that with solid testimony, and gain an understanding of what occurred. The following chapters include this data. If this is the first time you are reading about this event, I would expect you will need to reread many of the details and chapters a few times in order to gain a solid understanding.

The main objective of this text is to help anyone who is initially studying this topic to get a good grasp of what occurred. My personal background is Mechanical Engineering, with emphasis in the area of Engineering Analysis. Mechanical Engineers get involved in machinery and product design, thermal sciences like power generation and heat transfer, and some aspects of structural design. Emphasis in Engineering Analysis involves more details of the physics, stress analysis, computer programming, and computer simulations that support these areas of the larger group. In many cases, the true mathematics supporting the designs is generated thru Engineering Analysis techniques. For my review of the assassination, my focus is on presenting a more technical study on what occurred. Included in the text are technical reviews of some of the testimony and physical evidence. Where applicable, physical evidence is reviewed using dimensions, time frames, and angles. This approach develops a more technical review of this subject. Each chapter is ended with summary and conclusions that can be made from the preceding text. These items have resulted from my many years of reviewing the data and breaking down the complexity of this event. Once all the supporting conclusions are stated, I think an overall description of the event can shine thru.

In most complex crimes, the investigator can start to establish a convergence of the evidence. As each small piece of evidence is researched and analyzed, the true facts start to approach the big picture. Each small piece of evidence supports the final conclusion. In my Engineering practice, we periodically are asked to analyze a faulty piece of machinery. I see the same trend occurring in this exercise. As we solve a smaller problem of the entire system, we start to see how it fits into the overall running performance. Once you solve all these small puzzles, the larger puzzle ends up solving itself. With the assassination of JFK, we see the opposite. The more you think you solve a small detail, the support for the big picture tends to fan out and diverge. You find it frustrating and mysterious. This is why this event has captivated such a large audience over the many years. Many of the main characters are participants in mysterious and sometimes unexplained activities. The witnesses who were near the assassination have varying accounts of what they saw and heard, which leads to difficulty in establishing the facts.

This text is a summary of my effort to make sense of this event. I used the available documents, films, and testimony, along with the many hours spent by the previous researches, as my effort to tie the facts together. A complete list of these invaluable resources is located in the appendix of this text. Where possible, I applied my Engineering experience and knowledge to reach conclusions. Included, are selected figures and diagrams that relate to this subject matter. Most of these are from the National Archives or created by myself as an aid to present this material. Many of the figures and famous photographs cannot be duplicated in the book, but are easily found online. When referenced in the text, I encourage you to search for these pictures and videos while you are reading. I also encourage your feedback and would be happy to engage in open discussion. Please contact me at arantepublishing@gmail.com . Now it is time to move forward into the next chapters of this story. I hope you find the information enlightening and beneficial to your understanding of this event.

Chapter 1 – Overview

Lee Harvey Oswald would become the suspected lone assassin. His background and history by itself are both loaded with mystery and various unknowns. At a young age, he joined the marines. He held various assignments including an assignment in Japan. Later, he defected to Russia. He married in Russia and came back to the United States. He spent time in Dallas, New Orleans, and Mexico City. Much of what happened with Oswald just prior to the assassination has been researched and debated. The Mexico City trip is one example. The trip was just a few months prior to the assassination. While in Mexico City, he allegedly entered the US embassy. The sound recordings and photo evidence from the embassy surveillance captured him entering and calling the staff there. However, the photographed person and recorded voice does not match the Oswald we know. This is just one area of an overall story that by itself, has never been fully resolved. Oswald always seems to have strong political opinions and beliefs. However, at times they seemed to be conflicting in nature.

The day of the assassination, Oswald was an employee of the Texas School Book Depository (TSBD) located in downtown Dallas in a place called Dealey Plaza. The event took place on a Friday November 22, 1963 in Dallas Texas. The location of the assassination was in Dealey Plaza. The president was riding in an open limousine on his way from a main airport (Loves Field) to the Trade Mart Center. Several cars and police motorcycles were in the presidential motorcade, which drove thru the streets of Dallas. The time of the assassination was 12:30 local time. The weather in Dallas that day began as rain and then changed to be sunny.

Dealey Plaza is a unique section of Dallas that combines three roads that funnel into a section call the Triple Underpass. To get to the Trade Mart Center, the motorcade was chartered to drive along the northern branch of Dealey Plaza, which is a one way street called Elm street. Elm street runs in the west direction and includes several areas that have become very well known to researchers. Figure 1.1 shows a view of Dealey Plaza with some of these landmarks highlighted. In this picture, The Elm Street traffic is running from east to west to the Triple Underpass. The motorcade path was revised to include the sharp turn onto Elm so that it could eventually get onto the Stemmons Freeway. The Stemmons Freeway would bring the motorcade to the next stop which is the Trade Mart Center.

Figure 1.1 – Dealey Plaza – *courtesy of shutterstock 229796410*

The assassination occurred as the presidential limo proceeded north on Houston and then made the sharp left turn onto Elm Street. Right after this turn, the shots were heard with the final shot hitting president Kennedy in the head. The limo at this location was about half way between the corner of Houston and Elm, and the Triple Underpass. This is just the beginning of the story as the events that take place afterwards makes this event more and more complicated.

Just after hearing the shots, a Dallas police officer (Marion Baker) jumped off his motorcycle and ran into the Texas School Book Depository (TSBD). His feeling at the time of the shots was that they were high so he suspected one of the close by taller buildings. Once he left his motorcycle, he was joined by Roy Truly the building manager. The two men immediately ran to the building elevators so that they could quickly get to the roof. The elevators were both out of service at that time, so they used the only set of stairs to head to the top floors. On the second floor, Policeman Baker stopped because he saw a man in the lunch room. The stairway for this building is open on each floor, so Policeman Baker could see a great part of the floor as they passed. The man he saw was Lee Harvey Oswald who was in the second floor lunchroom. Policeman Baker ran to Oswald and confronted him with his weapon drawn. Later, both Baker and Truly would state that Oswald did not appear nervous or out of breath as they confronted him. Mr. Truly stated that Oswald was an employee of the TSBD, so they continued upward on the stairs. The time between the first audible shot and the meeting on the second floor was later determined to be about 90 seconds (1.1). Note that Oswald would quickly become the main suspect and the Dallas police would determine the shots came from the sixth floor of the TSBD.

This one event has been debated for years. The short time of 90 seconds is barely enough for someone to hide the gun, run down the stairs unnoticed and remain calm and composed. He maintained this posture as officer Baker pointed a revolver at his stomach. A big issue became whether or not Oswald had a coke in his hand during this encounter. He was standing in front of the lunchroom pop machine. If he just purchased a coke, it would take almost half of the 90 seconds to fish the change out of his pocket and put it into the machine. This could nail down his location during the time shots were fired to be in the lunch room. Other TSBD employees have testified he was in the area of the second floor just before the assassination took place. But if this is not enough to nail it down, the next event may be the defining moment.

Victoria Adams and Sandra Styles were watching the motorcade from the fourth floor of the TSBD (1.2). Just after the shots rang out, the two girls decided to follow the crowd heading up to the Grassy Knoll. Since the elevators were down, they ran to the one set of stairs. At the same time this occurred, Oswald would have been coming down from the sixth floor on these same stairs, had he indeed been on the sixth floor. During their time on the stairs, they did not see or hear Oswald. Another employee sitting near the stair entrance also did not see Oswald, but did see Baker and Truly shortly after Victoria and Sandra went down.

Most remarkable were the events taking place on the Grassy Knoll. At the same time as the above interactions, several people rushed up to the Grassy Knoll picket fence. Witnesses felt shots came from behind the fence at the top of the Grassy Knoll. Included with the bystanders was police officer Joe M. Smith (1.3). He was likely the first person to arrive. The officer dropped his motorcycle near the curb and ran up the hill seconds after the assassination took place. What he encountered is critical and shocking. From everything I learned about the assassination, the interaction between officer Joe Smith and the person he encountered is one of the single most remarkable events of this day. He encountered a secret service man who showed his ID and said "I have this area secure". Later investigations determined that the secret service had no agents in this area. They all stayed with the motorcade.

Malcolm Summers (1.4) ran from the south side of Elm Street to the east Knoll area and was stopped by a man with a raincoat over his arm. Under the coat, Malcolm saw the barrel of a gun. The man stated "you had better not come up here or you could get shot". Who were these men? Malcolm has told this story with absolute consistency for forty years. Why did these two men obstruct people getting behind the fence? These events occurred within seconds of the assassination and were never explained. Once I learned this, I realized that Oswald, if he was involved, was not the only participant. My attitude of wanting to learn about the event changed to one of suspecting the worst. JFK was likely assassinated in a conspiracy involving more than a single lone nut.

Later that day, Oswald was arrested in a theater and charged with killing a policeman. Officer Tippit was gunned down in a suburb of Dallas just after 1 pm. This occurred near a boarding house where Oswald rented a room. Each week, Oswald would stay in the boarding house which was only 3 miles from the TSBD. The location of the boarding house was Oak Cliff where Oswald rented a single room amongst several other residents. His wife and children stayed with Ruth Paine in Irving Texas. For the time that Oswald was working at the TSBD, he would only stay at the Paine's house on weekends. Oswald did not have a driver's license and did not own a car. When he travelled, it was typically by bus or taxi, or with another driver.

Ruth Paine must have been a great help to the Oswald family. She spoke fluent Russian which was the primary language Marina Oswald (Lee's wife) could speak. Marina had two small children at this time. Ruth Paine helped with the children and also was trying to teach Lee Oswald how to drive. Lee Oswald travelled to New Orleans in the summer of 1963, about 3 months before the assassination. This part of the story just does not make sense. Why did he go to New Orleans? His second daughter was born on October 20 and he was in New Orleans in August and September, a few months before his daughter's birth. What was his agenda and objective that needed to be addressed in New Orleans?

At the time of his apprehension, Oswald was strongly suspected of the JFK assassination, however, assassination charges were not formally made at that time. The actions of the Dallas police department and the press coverage was shocking. The Dallas police station was openly discussing the suspect and actually brought him out for a press conference. He proclaimed his innocence, continued asking for legal representation, and at one point angrily stated "I'm just a patsy!" Today, we could never expect this much openness around a major homicide. In most cases, the facts of the case are never discussed openly with the press. The investigators and police keep the detailed evidence confidential.

At the time of the assassination, I was six years old. We lived in a one flat unit located in Cicero Illinois. The kitchen, bedrooms, and living room were all on one level. I remembered my mom being upset that weekend like much of the nation was. My Dad was as well. I remember him watching our black and white TV with the nonstop news coverage. On Sunday morning, two days after the assassination, they were bringing Oswald out to transfer him to another prison. I was in the kitchen and my dad was in the living room. Then on live TV, Jack Ruby shot Oswald. I remember my dad screaming, "They shot him, they shot him on live TV!" And just like that, Oswald would no longer be able to talk. These are my first memories of the assassination. The events of these three days were shocking and profound. What came next in the subsequent investigation by our government has only added to the mystery.

Shortly after the assassination, the new president Lyndon Johnson assembled a commission to study the assassination. The commission was called the Warren Commission and was led by Earl Warren. Right from the start, the effort seemed to be on a predetermined agenda. Selective information was released to the public with much of it held under wraps as classified. In addition, witness testimony was very selective. Our government was determined to paint a picture that the assassination was the result of a single "lone nut". The information that came from the Dallas police seemed to be excessively open whereas the Federal Government was now being very selective about what would be released. Much of the underlying concern of the government was the fact that Lee Harvey Oswald had previously defected to Russia. If the public thought the assassination was a Russian plot, this country could have been drawn into serious conflict. If the Warren Commission could convince the world that the JFK assassination was due to a single lone nut, without anyone else involved, that would be the best scenario to put forth.

Compounding the narrow focus of the Warren Commission and the enormous amount of information that was held back as classified, key witnesses mysteriously started to die. During the assassination, Lee Bowers was behind the picket fence in the railroad tower. He was an employee of the Union Terminal Company responsible for switching and logistics. His view point was elevated in the tower where he could observe cars entering and leaving the parking area. He also had a good view of the back side of the picket fence. He saw strange activity including people under the tree at the corner of the fence. This is very strange since if someone wanted to see the motorcade, it would be a much closer and better view to stand on the curb as the motorcade drives by. There was plenty of space at this time since the crowds along the route really thinned out in this area. Lee Bowers died mysteriously shortly thereafter. This is just one example of many. As key witnesses were being called for testimony, they would suddenly die prior to their arrival.

Figure 1.2 – Railroad Tower – *courtesy of arantepublishing*

For many years, I struggled with the facts and data surrounding the assassination. After reading several books and watching several films, I could never resolve many of the key data points. In 1979, I graduated college with a degree in Mechanical Engineering and took a job as an Engineering Analyst. The specialty of Engineering Analysis used mathematics and computer simulations to support the design of structures and machinery. I always had an analytical approach and felt most complex events can be solved and answered by analytical approaches. My analysis of this event is presented in the following chapters. There are so many aspects to this case, you could spend a lifetime trying to investigate the open ends. In many cases, the information available about this event does not provide answers, but tends to just lead to more questions. I tried to focus on the evidence that *can* be fully analyzed and maintained my focus where conclusions *can* be drawn. In many cases, I used the information from previous researchers. Where applicable, additional references are noted. Throughout this text, I added my observations and conclusions. I hope you find this information helpful in answering the questions related to that event in 1963.

SUMMARY and CONCLUSIONS

1) This case is complicated and involves multiple critical events. It has been 58 years, and still many critical and crucial parts of the story are still not fully understood.

2) In addition to being complicated, this case has a lot of information with many back stories. You can research one aspect of the case and find a tremendous amount of information. For example, the story of Victoria Adams (1.2) is a very critical sub story within the bigger picture.

3) Oswald was likely not located on the sixth floor of the TSBD during the assassination.

4) The secret service agents on the ground in Dealey Plaza were never identified.

5) The timing of Oswald's trip to New Orleans seems inappropriate with the birth of his daughter right around the corner. Furthermore, I could never understand how this travel was financed since he was unemployed prior to the trip.

6) The Warren Commission's charter was to show the world a single lone nut was

responsible for the JFK assassination, rather than really to determine what occurred and who did what.

7) Watching the motorcade from behind the picket fence does not make any sense when there was plenty of space at the curbside. Whatever Lee Bowers saw behind the fence was malfeasance in nature.

Chapter 2 – Prior Knowledge

Whether or not the JFK assassination was caused by an isolated "lone nut" or by a group is one of the key open issues of this case. If a group had planned this event, more than one person would be involved. Some key events occurred prior to the assassination that indicate prior knowledge. If we find an isolated case of prior knowledge, that may be explained away as coincidence. However, when multiple cases occur, it becomes harder to say it is just a coincidence. The following events refer to details that occurred prior to November 22, 1963, the date of the assassination.

Rose Cherami (2.1) was travelling to Dallas a few days before November 22, 1963. She was with two other men. Their journey started in Florida. The objective of this trip was related to picking up some drugs. Along the way, a disagreement ended with Rose being separated from the men. She was found on the side of the road on November 20th after being struck by a car. This occurred close to Eunice Louisiana. After being brought to a hospital, she told several people that the two men she had been travelling with were on their way to Dallas to "kill the president". She spent the weekend in the hospital bed and became aware of the killing of JFK, and then the killing of Oswald by Jack Ruby. She then said that she knew both Oswald and Ruby and stated they knew each other. This information was reported by Louisiana police Lieutenant Francis Fruge. It is well documented and very credible. . . but was never fully investigated. Rose Cherami died on September 4, 1965 from injuries to her head. This was the result of getting hit by a car near Big Sandy Texas.

Richard Case Nagell (2.2) had prior knowledge of the JFK assassination and also knew Lee Harvey Oswald. The above referenced book is an excellent story about the very complex history of both these men. Nagell worked with government intelligence. Prior plans to assassinate JFK are presented in this book. This book outlines, in detail, the possible group activities behind the assassination.

Aubrey Rike was an ambulance driver in Dallas at the time of the assassination. He would later be the last person to handle JFK's body before it was removed from Dallas. At 12:20 that day, someone fainted in the crowd gathering at Dealey Plaza. This was 10 minutes prior to the assassination. Aubrey was called and had transported the patient to Parkland hospital. Aubrey was there when the trauma team responded to the motorcade. In the weeks prior to the presidential visit and motorcade, Aubrey noted that several calls were made for medical emergencies in Dealey Plaza. All were made at midday and all were determined to be false alarms with no one there. This indicates someone may have been timing the response for ambulances to get to Dealey plaza. Maybe this was an attempt to test an ambulance arrival in Dealey Plaza in order to have an impact on the motorcade movement.

Eugene Dinkin was ranked as an army private first class while stationed in Metz France. His duties included cryptographic code operation. On November 6, 1963, he stated there was a plot against JFK scheduled for November 28 in Dallas. Dinkin was arrested and placed in psychiatric care.

Recently, president Trump approved the release of JFK documents that had been classified and sealed. One of the documents describes a call made to the Cambridge News, a British local newspaper. This call was documented in a CIA memo that had been locked up since the assassination. The memo states that they should call the American embassy in London for some big news. The British intelligence group MI5 calculated the memo as 25 minutes prior to the assassination.

All these events are documented and point to prior knowledge of the JFK assassination. Combine these details with the "no secret service on the Grassy Knoll" scenario and it does support a conspiracy over a "lone nut" assassination. Whether or not Oswald was part of it, or a patsy, still needs to be determined. As noted above, one episode of "prior knowledge" does not close the case. However, when multiple cases emerge, the probability starts to move in the direction of conspiracy.

Forensic Engineering is the study of applying Engineering principles and Engineering Analysis to identify the root cause of failure. In some cases, this approach is taken to help understand machinery performance. A case of applying Forensic Engineering could be the following. Assume an automation device (i.e., robot) is used to move material. It would likely require a motion from the pickup station to the drop off location. If this motion is erratic with vibration and bounce, that tells us that an issue exists with the design and/or assembly. The components of this design, in part or combined, have possible defects which includes wear or premature failure. Continuing to run this piece of equipment in this way will only lead to a failure and downtime. In our quest to correct this situation, we gather data and apply Engineering Analysis. When completed, we typically identify the most probable root causes. In most cases, our conclusions relate to a series of possible issues rather than a single isolated area. It is very rare that a malfunctioning piece of equipment has only one area that needs to be repaired.

In the same way we try to draw these conclusions for our faulty machine, the true crime investigation searches for data to support or reject a theory. Searching for the definite proof is the search for the "smoking gun". This phrase is used to describe a scenario where the murderer is caught red handed and still holding the weapon. In difficult cases, the true definite proof or smoking gun is never found. For our case here, we do not have anything that resembles the smoking gun. However, we can start to look at probabilities. When more and more cases of prior knowledge are found, the probability of conspiracy goes up.

Many of the witnesses around the JFK assassination have died mysteriously (2.3). As the number of deaths have increased, the suspicion of conspiracy has grown. This is another area where we use probability to help understand what has happened. The probability that these deaths are unrelated to the assassination becomes very low to the point of being impossible (2.4).

SUMMARY and CONCLUSIONS

1) The story of Rose Cherami is an important part of this case. This should have been investigated by the Warren Commission while she was alive. Her prior knowledge of the event together with her insinuation that she knew Oswald and Ruby should have been looked at closer and early on in the assassination investigation.

2) As the cases of prior knowledge stack up, it tends to support a conspiracy.

3) One aspect that makes this case so difficult is that there is no definite "smoking gun" for either guilt or innocence of Oswald.

Chapter 3 – Texas School Book Depository and Dealey Plaza

As The Warren Commission completed their review of the assassination evidence, internal problems developed. Probably the most specific case of these problems is the development of the Single Bullet Theory. This will be detailed later in this text. The Warren Commission concluded that three shots were fired from a bolt action rifle from the sixth floor of the TSBD. Evidence on the sixth floor includes Oswald's rifle and three shell casings on the floor. The area where the casings were found included stacked boxes at the south east window. The boxes looked to create a rifle rest or possibly a barrier as if to isolate the activity at the window ledge. Throughout the years, this corner of the sixth floor TSBD has been referred to as the "sniper's nest". Although the sniper's nest evidence looked to support three shots, the number of bullet wounds, wound location, and other details did not conclusively support only three shots.

Several years ago, I visited Dealey Plaza. The sixth floor of the TSBD is now a museum. The arrangements at the sixth floor south east corner (sniper's nest) are isolated under glass. The box arrangements and window opening are preserved as they were found that day. Please refer to pictures of the Texas School Book

Depository sixth floor sniper's nest online, in order to get a better understanding of what was found. The lower part of the window frame is only about 12 to 16 inches from the floor. The window itself is half opened with the lower sill of the sliding portion just about in line with the top surface of the shorter stack of boxes. Photographic evidence confirms this window was half open during the assassination. The space on top of the short stack of boxes and the lower ledge of the sliding window is too small to allow for a rifle with a scope. The rifle would need to be supported on the lower sill of the frame, which is 12-16 inches from the floor line. If shots came out of this window, there was no space to view the target with the weapon supported on top of these boxes. The open viewing only gets more constricted at steeper rifle angles.

The short stack of boxes on the sill were always described as a gun rest. Hitting a moving target would require a solid rest to support and aim the rifle. The problem is, the line up with a target moving below on the street is just not there. The rifle lineup would be subject to interference with the sliding portion of the window, specifically the lower sill. Remember that the scope is on the top of the rifle and the view must be unobstructed. It would be difficult to view the target thru the window glass with any kind of accuracy. I think a shooter using this area would need to lie on the floor, or at least kneel with gun resting on the bottom opening of the window frame. Using the stacked boxes as a gun rest with the half open window does not line up with targets on the street below.

The windows in the upper floors of the TSBD are close to the floor (about 12 to 16 inches as noted above). From the street, this ledge looks like a typical window at waist height. But it is not. Since the empty bullet casings were found in the sniper's nest, it was always assumed the shots came from that area. The sixth floor is one continuous area with all the windows in the same room. The window in the south west corner had a wide open window during the assassination. This window looks to be a better location to shoot from. The shooter could stand back from the open window ledge in an upright position, rest the rifle on a taller stack of boxes, and aim at the target with an unobstructed view point. Note that the last statement just refers to the sixth floor characteristics combined with the window conditions at that time, and does not refer to wound locations or other ballistic evidence. If indeed shots came from the south west, wide open window, the angles from this window would tend to traverse the target more than from the south east window. Wound locations and paths would not be from front to back, but they would be across the bodies in a left to right direction. There are several pictures and films online that show the state of windows before and after the shots were fired. These pictures show the condition of both windows on the sixth floor.

When visiting the sixth floor, you can view the tree obstruction directly below together with the various streets around the building. Elm street is directly below the sixth floor. You can also see the very clear view of Houston Street, which does look like a much easier shot. Remembering the path of the motorcade, it first travelled down Houston and made the hairpin turn onto Elm. If the target is moving towards you on Houston, the movement is much less than going away on Elm. The vector of the car motion on Houston is almost directly towards you. Once the car turns onto Elm, the target is now proceeding from left to right and away, which makes it more of a moving target.

Elm street today includes a large white "X" that shows the president's location at the time of the head shot. The "X" is located about half way between the corner of Houston and Elm, and the Triple Underpass. Projecting back on the street from this point would be the limo location of the prior shots. Seeing this with my own eyes made me realize that shooting a single bullet through both Kennedy and Connelly in these prior locations was an impossibility. The angle is way too steep. Along with the restrictive open space of the window, shooting from the sniper's nest seems improbable.

My first impression of Dealey Plaza is that the buildings and monuments did not look nearly as large as everything does in the many films I had seen. The distance from the street level to the sixth floor of the TSBD is about 60 feet. The overall building height is 94 feet. Everything seems a lot smaller and more contained within a closer proximity. The typical filming of Dealey Plaza uses a panoramic view that makes everything look bigger. Along Houston Street, there are several large buildings similar in height to the TSBD. Any of these buildings could contain shooting locations. The point made above about the target movement being less on Houston than on Elm, for shooting locations in the TSBD, is the opposite for the buildings on Houston. As the limousine is moving on Houston, the target appears to move left to right as viewed form a building on Houston. Once the limousine completes the hairpin turn onto Elm, the target is now moving away from your viewing angle in a building on Houston. The target has less movement if you are in a building on Houston and you are aiming down Elm Street. Also, the tree obstruction is not there.

During my visit, I was able to walk behind the Grassy Knoll fence. Please refer to figure 1.1 if you are not familiar with the Grassy Knoll location. This area in Dealey Plaza has always been a suspected area for a shooter. The area is slightly elevated from the street and provides a much easier get away than being in an upper floor of a building. As I walked around in this area, my immediate conclusion was that no one who wanted to see the motorcade would view it from that point of view. There was plenty of space up close and on the Elm Street curb. If you were there to see the president, why not get a closer view of the motorcade? The pictures and films of that day indicate only a handful of people were on the curb in that area.

SUMMARY and CONCLUSIONS

1) Using the boxes in the sniper's nest for rigidly supporting and aiming the rifle at a downward angle together with the half open window does not allow for an un obstructed view.

2) Prior shots (before the head shot), when the limousine is closer to the corner of Houston and Elm, have a downward angle approaching 45 degrees.

3) Walking behind the picket fence confirms my thinking that whoever was back there during the assassination likely did not want to be seen, rather than wanting to see the motorcade.

Chapter 4 - Bullet Wounds

Key evidence in a murder investigation typically includes a thorough examination of the body. The body shows us the bullet trajectory, entrance and exit points, and in some scenarios, the physical evidence of the bullet slug. This information is typically gathered at a formal autopsy of the body. All this is typical, but for this case, nothing follows the typical procedures.

After JFK was pronounced dead at Parkland Memorial Hospital in Dallas, the next step should have been the formal autopsy. What happened in the assassination sequence, is the following events. The body was taken from the hospital by the secret service. This did not happen without resistance. The proper procedure should have been to let the body remain in Dallas under the control of Earl Rose the chief medical examiner and official Dallas coroner. Rose put up a fight, but the secret service maintained their posture and removed the body to load it on Air Force One.

The path the body took at this point is filled with even more mystery. Air Force One was headed to Bethesda Navy Hospital located in Bethesda Maryland. Once the plane landed, the casket was removed and transported to the Hospital using a small motorcade. However, to this day, this whole episode appears to be a facade. Once the casket arrived at the Bethesda autopsy room, several differences were noted. The body was removed from an ordinary transport shipping casket. Previously in Dallas, JFK was placed in a formal ornate casket as can be clearly seen in the various film coverage. In addition, the body at Bethesda was removed and taken out of crash bag with a zipper. In Dallas, the body was wrapped in several sheets prior to being placed in the ornate casket. Additional conflicts with evidence were soon to mount as the body proceeded thru the autopsy. Wound descriptions and locations from Parkland doctors were different than what was now being cataloged. Two excellent references about this part of the story are (4.1, 4.2).

The following table shows our best attempt to create a summary of the wounds that occurred in Dealey Plaza. The sequence of the shots does not necessarily follow the wound number. The description briefly describes the wounds with a most probably direction of entrance.

No	Person	Description
1	JFK	Throat, front entrance
2	JFK	Back, rear entrance did not exit
3	John Connally	Back wound, thru chest into right wrist, out of the wrist, into the right thigh. Rear entrance, no exit in thigh
4	James Tague	Received a cut to the face from a bullet deflection
5	JFK	Head, front entrance with exit thru the rear

Figure 4.1 Wound Summary – *arantepublishing*

Additional information about each of the wounds is listed here.

1) The throat wound was first seen in Parkland hospital. This wound was described as small in diameter which in ballistics is characteristic of an entrance wound. As noted above, the body was not fully examined until it arrived at Bethesda. However, several of the doctors and nurses reported an additional large wound in the back of the head. In ballistics, the large opening indicates a point of exit.

2) This wound is described by James Jenkins in (4.2) and also in some of his excellent YOUTUBE interviews. He described the wound as entering the back (between T2 and T3) at a 25-30 degree downward angle, and then stopping before entering the lung cavity. His description is very detailed. The wound probing was done by doctor Pierre Finck who was one of the more senior autopsy doctors at Bethesda for the JFK autopsy. Jenkins observed the probing from the front side of JFK.

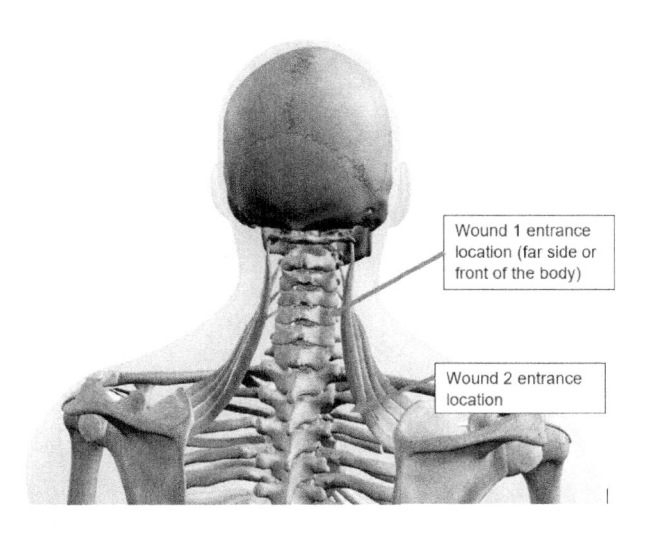

[Wound 1 entrance location (far side or front of the body)]

[Wound 2 entrance location]

Figure 4.2 Back view of vertebrate with wound markings
courtesy of shutterstock
1800822229

3) John Connally describes the events and the point at which he was wounded in great detail. His description is captured in several interviews and testimony. In the limousine, he was positioned directly in front of JFK. He heard the first shot, turned to his right, could not see JFK, and then started to turn back to his left. When he reached close to the front position, he was hit in the back. Over the years, he repeated this description several times and has been very consistent.

The seating arrangements for the limousine is well documented and can be seen in several photographs online. The front seat included the secret service driver and a second agent located in the passenger seat. The back seat included JFK on the passenger side and the first lady Jackie Kennedy on the driver's side. Between these two areas is a jump seat that can be left down or up. In this case, it includes Governor John Connally on the passenger side and his wife Nellie Connally on the driver's side. From this description, you can see that John Connally is directly in front of JFK and Nellie Connally is in front of Jackie.

4) James Tague was located under the triple underpass (see figure 1.1). He was not directly hit with a bullet, but did receive a facial wound from a deflection. The curb near where he was standing had a fresh mark on it. The conclusion was that this bullet totally missed the limousine and hit the curb.

5) The shot that hit JFK in the head appears to be a front entrance (4.4). The momentum of his body is from front to rear. This will be discussed later in the text.

Single Bullet Theory

The Warren Commission created the Single Bullet Theory in order to compact the assassination to three shots fired in a six second time frame. The six second time frame was derived from the weapon type and the film evidence taken in Dealey Plaza. The theory they presented is that one bullet entered JFK's upper back below the hairline, exited thru the throat and then on to Governor John Connally entering into his back, out thru his chest, thru his wrist, and then into his thigh. A bullet was found at the hospital that matched Oswald's rifle and the theory was expanded to say this was the single bullet. The bone damage to Connally clearly does not match the damage to the bullet. Further development of this theory stated the first shot was deflected to eventually wound James Tague and that the second shot fired was the "single bullet".

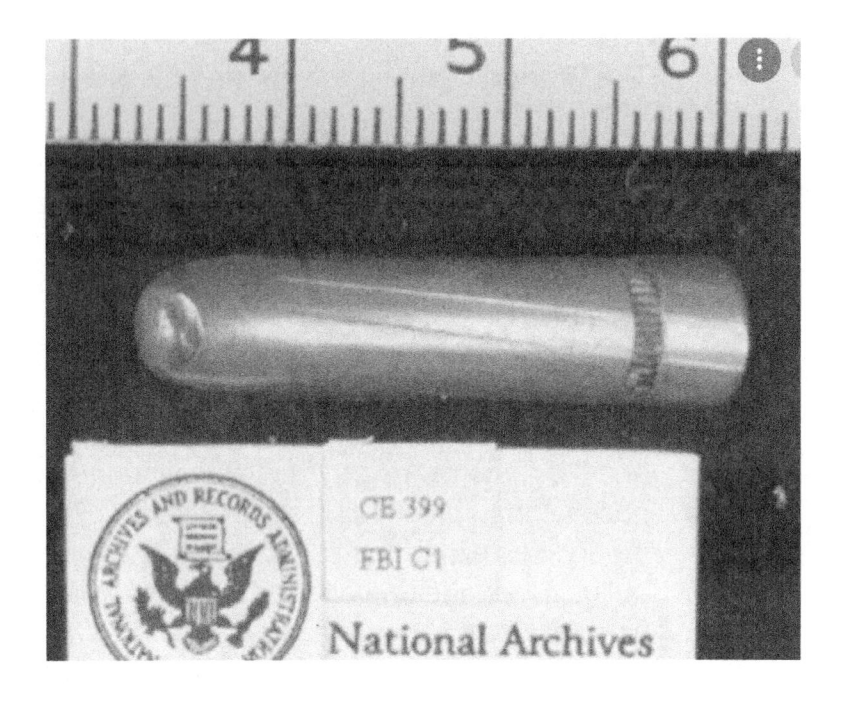

Figure 4.3 Actual bullet found at Parkland hospital – *courtesy of the National Archives Commission Exhibit (CE) 399*

This bullet (figure 4.3) was found in the above condition and appears to be in too good of shape to have caused the bone damage. To demonstrate this further, the following figure 4.4 is from the Warren Commission ballistic tests. The testing used the same ammunition that would be used in Oswald's rifle. The figure shows the Parkland hospital bullet (CE399) together with some samples under various firing scenarios.

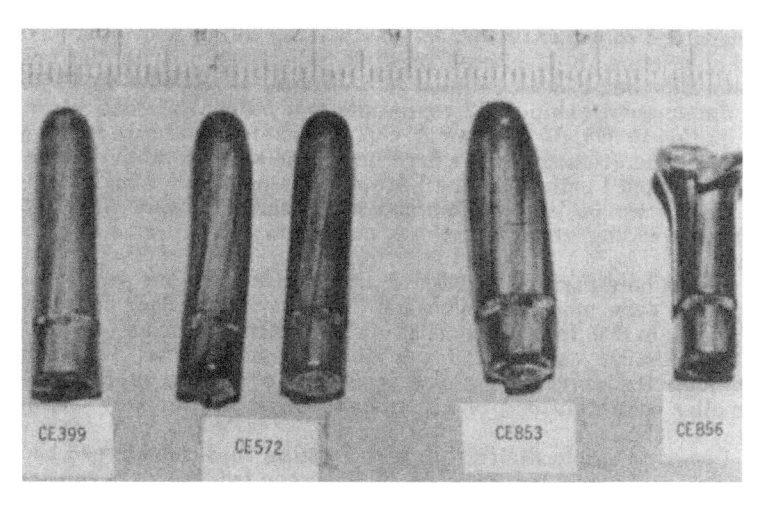

Figure 4.4 Warren Commission ballistic test exhibits CE572, CE853, and CE856 Compared to the Parkland Hospital bullet CE399 – *courtesy of the National Archives*

The results of the Warren Commission test are as follows. Bullets CE572 were fired thru cotton wadding hitting no rigid obstacles. Bullet CE853 broke one goat rib. Bullet CE856 broke the distal end of the wrist radius bone in a human cadaver. Note that John Connally had several broken bones as a result of his wounds, which included his ribs and the large bone in his wrist.

Dr. Cyril Wecht is an American forensic pathologist. He is an expert in this area of criminal science and has been involved in many critical high profile murders. He was involved in the JFK assassination and the Warren Commission from the very start. He was always a critic of the Single Bullet Theory with his emphasis towards the improbable bullet trajectories and the condition of the bullet found at Parkland hospital. Many times, he held up the slide in figure 4.4 and said, "if I had to use one slide to show my disagreement with the Single Bullet Theory, this is it". The condition of the bullet on the far right that broke one bone stands in contrast with the bullet found in Parkland that was allegedly responsible for breaking several bones. On top of that point, this slide was developed by the Warren Commission, who are the very people arguing that CE399 did all the damage in Governor Connally after passing thru JFK.

Trying to line up the single bullet with the back entry wound of JFK and the entry into the back of Connally is another challenge when you try and argue for the Single Bullet Theory. Several problems arise since a back entry from the sixth floor of the TSBD requires a downward trajectory. Starting at the wound location on JFK's back, it becomes too low to exit thru JFK's neck and then onward into Connally's torso. More discussion about the trajectory of the angles will be covered later in the text.

SUMMARY and CONCLUSIONS

1) The backwound description by James Jenkins is very detailed and very crucial to understanding the facts of the assassination. The entry point of this wound and the fact that it did not exit rules it out from being part of the Single Bullet Theory.

2) The bullet found in Parkland Hospital could not have done the damage to John Connally which included several broken bones.

3) Trying to describe the assassination wounds with three bullets is not practical. The number of entrance wounds is at least 4, likely 5 or even more. The shot that caused a deflection and hit James Tague (number 4) is a single missed shot. The back wound to JFK (number 2) did not exit. The head wound (number 5) is a separate shot as seen in the Zapruder film (to be discussed later). This adds up to three. We still have the throat wound to JFK and the Connally wounds that need to be accounted for.

Chapter 5 - Zapruder Film

During the assassination, several films captured the event. By far, the most detailed and valuable to researches is the Zapruder film. Abraham Zapruder and his receptionist Marilyn Sitzman stood on a concrete pillar in front of the grassy knoll area. While Marilyn held him in position, Zapruder filmed the entire movement of the motorcade on Elm Street. Please refer to the Mary Moorman Photo (5.1) online. This is taken just before the head shoot. In the background, Abraham Zapruder and Marilyn Sitzman can be seen standing on the monument column.

The Zapruder film can be seen on YOUTUBE with several enhancements and various speeds. For this text, I will be presenting selected frames from this film. The duration of the film covered the entire time shots were fired, with the final head shot most vividly captured. Zapruder was only about 35 feet away when the final head shot took place. The film was finally made available for public viewing in 1975. During the head shot, everyone noticed JFK's head snap back and his body fall to his left shortly after the shot.

The Zapruder film is a key piece of evidence and also serves as a timeline of the events. Each fame is a single picture exposure of that moment in time and has been assigned a number (i.e., Z210...Z313). These frame numbers are referred to by researchers. The film is now available in digital form and is available on the internet.

In addition to capturing the assassination frame by frame, the film also gives us an accurate time scale. The number of frames per second for the camara that Zapruder was using is 18.3. Each frame of the film occurs in .055 seconds. Once 18.3 frames have been exposed, one second of time has expired. Putting all this information together, we can capture the shooting details observed in the frames of the Zapruder film in real time.

The weapon found on the sixth floor of the TSBD, is a bolt action rifle and was determined to be purchased by Oswald. The way this rifle works is as follows. With one cartridge in the chamber, the shot is fired. During the shot, the bullet is projected from the rifle and the shell remains in the chamber. The next step is to eject the spent shell and load a new cartridge. To do this, the right hand is taken off the trigger and the bolt action knob is grabbed and cycled back to pop the old spent shell out. The motion to pop the old spent shell out requires to first move the knob up and then back. The bolt action knob is then cycled forward to load a new cartridge, and finally moved down. Next, the right hand is moved back to the trigger and the weapon is re-aligned thru the scope for the next shot.

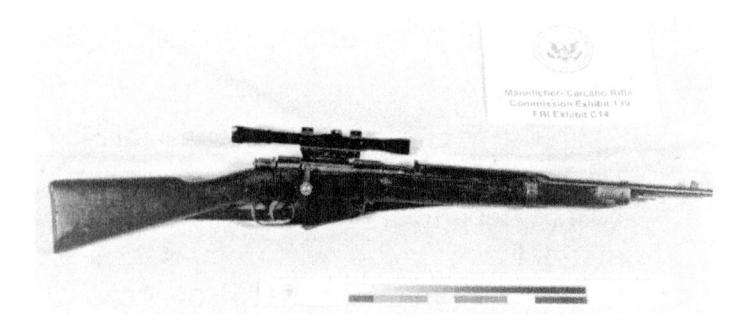

Figure 5.1 Oswald's Mannlicher-Carcano –
courtesy of the National Archives

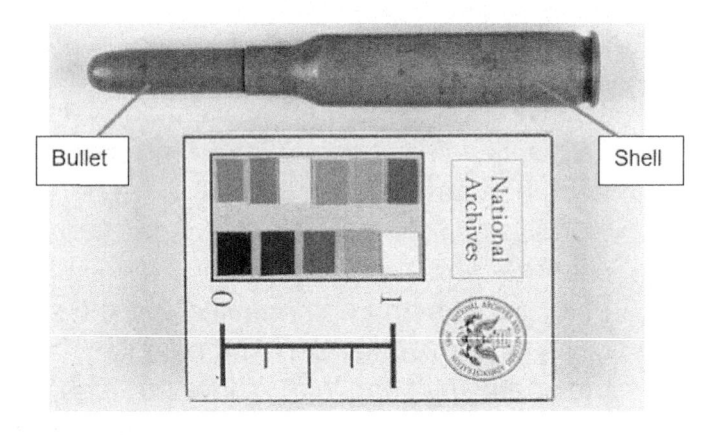

Figure 5.2 Rifle ammunition cartridge –
courtesy of the National Archives

The amount of time to use this weapon was studied and tested in order to establish the minimum time required between shots. The results of all the testing resulted in a time frame of 2.5 to 3 seconds between shots. Using this data with the Zapruder film, we can determine the following: It would take a minimum of 5 to 6 seconds to get off three shots which equates to 91 to 109 frames of the Zapruder film. This should be regarded as a minimum time estimate for this to occur. If more time is needed to zero in on the moving target, than the cycle time increased. If indeed three shots were fired, then the total time is at least 5 to 6 seconds.

When studying the Zapruder film, it is typical to start with the head shot frame and work backwards. This is typically regarded as the last shot of the assassination, no matter where it originated from. This frame number is Z313.

Figure 5.3 Zapruder Frame 313 (Z313) – *courtesy of the National Archives*

Following this shot, the presidents head snaps back as shown in the next figure. The frame shown in figure 5.4 is Z319 which is .33 seconds after the first evidence of the head shot. The body has clearly moved towards the back.

Figure 5.4 Z319 – *courtesy of the National Archives*

Whether or not we should expect his head to snap back on a shot from the front or the rear, has been forever debated. I think to really understand this, we should first think about the position of JFK's body just prior to the head shot. He is in the process of holding his neck and he is sitting up from his seat such that there is a gap between his back and the limousine seat. Upon getting hit in the head, his body reacts to the momentum of the impact. Since he is not supported in the back at this time. He receives a force at about a three foot moment arm to his thighs. This is a torque that he has no back support to resist. If he had been against the back seat at the time, the motion would have been more constrained to his head. The motion is pronounced and results from momentum due to a frontal impact. Had the shot came from the rear, I would expect Z319 to show JFK moving towards the back of the seat in front of him, to the point where he is falling off his seat.

I have seen samples of skulls supported on springs where people have tried to argue the motion is backward on a rear shot. In one particular example, the skull is supported on a 2 inch spring that is fixed at the base of the spring. This is not a representation of the actual situation. JFK was up from the back rest as noted above, such that the center of the impact created a torque with a three foot moment arm. This is an important difference. Also, using a spring in that simulation is totally inaccurate. The spring stores potential energy that would release after the event.

To resolve any doubt about this motion, I think about an experiment we did back when I was in college. It was a physics experiment that was part of the chapter studies regarding momentum and the response of impact of objects. In addition to studying the response of pool balls and the impact using air tables, we did the experiment call the Ballistic Pendulum. The experiment involved a 4 by 4 wooden block that was supported from above. The support included two cables and the block was about 10 inches long. We had a rifle that was securely mounted in front of the block. The instructor fired a bullet into the block (see figure 5.5). Once the bullet was fired, the block movement was tracked in order to establish the resulting angle of swing. Using the pendulum motion equations together with the bullet and block mass, we had to solve the equations for the movement. The block swung away from the direction of fire about 30 to 45 degrees. The time for this motion to occur was within a second and occurred after the shot was fired. The bullet was trapped about half way thru the block. Had the bullet trajectory just made it out of the block, the motion would still be in the same direction. The reduction of bullet velocity means the transfer of energy is moving from the bullet mass to the combined mass of the block and bullet. This energy translates to a motion which is away from the direction of fire.

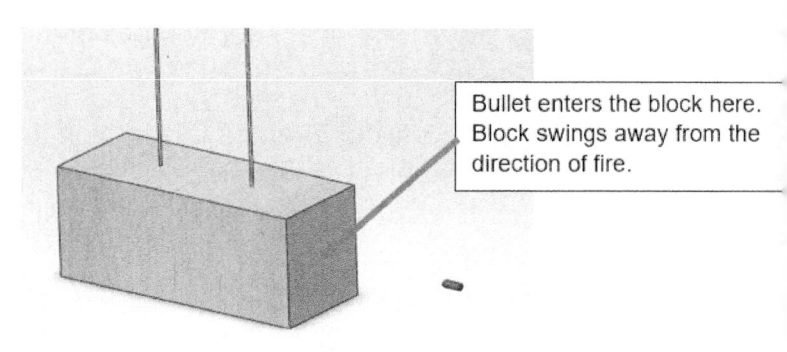

Figure 5.5 The Ballistics Pendulum experiment – *arantepublishing*

Another argument for rear motion on a rear entry is the blood pressure rocket propulsion theory. The argument that the blood pressure leaving the body created a thrust to move the head backward is also not practical. The maximum pressure in the blood stream is typically 120 mHg. This is the systolic reading of your blood pressure. Equating this to pounds per square inch (psi) gives 2.3 psi. For comparison, note that the typical air pressure in your car tire is around 30 psi. The pressure thrust argument is trying to equate this to rocket propulsion. Rocket propulsion requires about a 1000 psi or more, and it must be sustained to create the liftoff. This argument does not represent an actual characteristic of the event.

The blood splatter that we see in Z313 (Zapruder frame 313) is much better understood in today's criminal science. When the bullet enters the body, we get a fanning out of blood and matter around the entry point. This description is covered in detail in reference (5.2). In close contact as if someone was shot within a foot or two, the assailant will get hit with the blood splatter as the body is falling away. This fact is used in some cases where the murderer is in close proximity to the victim. In these scenarios, the assassin will contain evidence of the victim's blood splatter. Although we do not have this condition in the JFK assassination, we do clearly see the blood splatter phenomenon as we look at Zapruder frame 313.

Using the location of the head shot and a plan view of Dealey plaza we can project the position of the limousine movement during the time shots were fired. This assumes the last shot is the head shot. In figure 5.6, we can see Zapruder frame 200. This is 113 frames before head shot which equates to 6.2 seconds. At this point, the limousine is completely covered and we cannot see JFK or John Connally.

Figure 5.6 Z200 – *courtesy of the National Archives*

The view is blocked by the Stemmons freeway sign. This sign is not present in Dealey Plaza today, however, at that time, it created a temporary viewing barrier for the Zapruder film. Note that the frames prior to this show the four principal occupants in the limousine waving and smiling to the people lined up on both sides of the street.

The first reactions to the gunfire occur shortly after Z200. Advancing to the next frames, we can see reactions from JFK and Jackie Kennedy. In figure 5.7, JFK is clutching his neck and Jackie is now looking directly at him. Both JFK and Jackie have realized something is wrong.

Figure 5.7 Z224 – *courtesy of the National Archives*

This is a physical reaction by both JFK and Jackie. These reactions do not occur instantaneously, but will take at least .2 to .3 seconds. This equates to about 4 to 5 Zapruder frames. JFK is likely reacting to a neck or back shot that occurred at about Z200, or even slightly prior. Recall that the wounds we could identify are summarized in the previous chapter.

The physical reaction scenario is common when any pain or stimulus occurs to a person. It takes a certain amount of time for the body to determine pain has occurred and a physical reaction next takes place. If you reach into an oven that is at 400 °F and accidently touch the hot rack surface, your body tells you "this is too hot, I need to pull my hand out". This sequence will take .2 to .3 seconds and you will be left with a small burn mark.

During this same time of the reactions by JFK and Jackie, John Connally can be observed. Figure 5.8 shows a close up of the frames 222 thru 224.

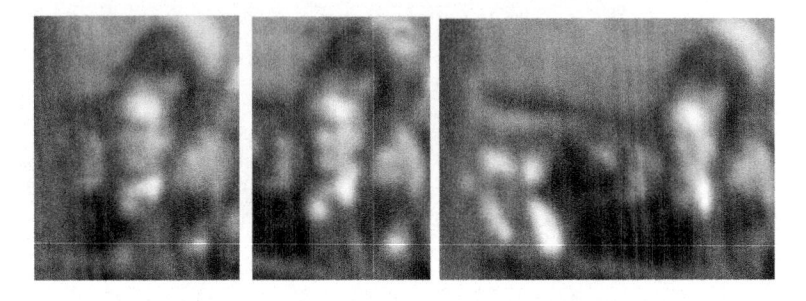

Figure 5.8 Z222, Z223, and Z224, close-up of John Connally – *courtesy of the National Archives*

Note that in 224, the lapel of his jacket is pushed out and his checks are puffed. This is a physical occurrence rather than a reaction by Connally. This happens in real time as the bullet is passing thru him. His lung was collapsed when the shot hit him causing his checks to puff out. Note that as early as Z222, Jackie is focused on JFK to see what is wrong.

The next three frames are shown below.

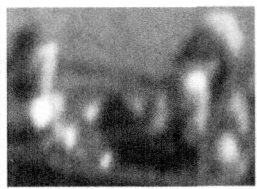

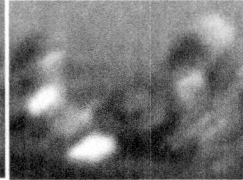

Figure 5.9 Z225, Z226, and Z227 – *courtesy of the National Archives*

The likely frame number that John Connally was hit is Z224. The reaction to the momentum of the shot moves his body forward by Z227. Looking at these two shots, the first to JFK and the second to Connally, they likely occurred at Z200 and Z224, respectively. These must be two separate shots and they are spaced about 24 frames (1.32 seconds) apart. This is not enough time to cycle the bolt action of the Oswald weapon.

In particular, anyone who looks at frame Z224 and says "see the bullet just pass thru Connally and JFK has just been hit. You can see all this in the single frame!" This is just not correct. The muzzle velocity for a rifle is about 2000 Feet per second. For our Zapruder time scale, the bullet travels about 110 feet for each frame. Any bullet path that is identified in a Zapruder frame has just left the weapon in that same frame. I believe

Connally was not hit before Z224, and most likely on Z224. JFK and Jackie are clearly reacting to the previous shot that hit JFK. It cannot be the same bullet for all the reasons stated above.

Additional critical information supports the theory of multiple shots, which is the testimony of John and Nellie Connally (ref 4.3 and 5.3). John Connally has clearly stated that he recognized the first noise as a gunshot, he turned to his right to see JFK behind him, he reached a point where he still could not see him, then he was turning back to try and turn to his left. When he was close to centrally positioned, he felt a blow to his back. He always thought he was hit by a second shot which he acknowledged he did not hear. Nellie recognized the first shot as a gunshot. She turned and first noticed JFK grabbing his neck. She has described this as a rigid fact with no wavering. Following that, her husband was hit. At that time, all her attention was directed to John and trying to stop his bleeding. She was successful in saving John Connally's life.

None of the above information can support a Single Bullet Theory. It is just impossible. In addition, the angle of the bullet trajectory during these shots is too steep to be originated from the TSBD sixth floor sniper's nest. The height of the TSBD is 94 feet. The sniper's nest is located at about 60 feet. At this moment in time, the limousine was located about 80 feet from the southeast corner of the TSBD. The angle from the window of the sniper's nest, or south east corner of the TSBD is 37 degrees with the horizontal. This angle is too steep. If we project this vector to some of the other tall buildings in close proximity (i.e., located on Houston Street), then various angles of trajectory will be produced.

In an effort to get angles to line up, researchers will move wound and seat locations a few degrees or inches and show a line up with the sniper's nest. We need to be careful when accepting this argument. Note that a few inches of relocation in the limousine translates to several floors and windows on the TSBD, or any other of the close by buildings for that matter. The pivot point is typically assumed to be the entry to JFK. Connally is a few feet in front of JFK. One foot of relocation on Connally produces a change on the face of the TSBD of 26 feet. See figure 5.10 below to help understand the projection.

Figure 5.10 – Angle projections – *courtesy of shutterstock 4005818*

Unless we have exact location information with very tight tolerances, the projection to the TSBD floor and other buildings is difficult. Trying to offset the wound locations between JFK and Connally for the purpose of showing a line up with the sniper's nest is too easy to create misinformation. This was first attempted by Arlen Specter, who created the Single Bullet Theory for the Warren Commission. Bottom line, however, is the angle seams too steep when you stand up on the sixth floor and you line up your site with the actual limousine location at that time.

For any murder investigation, the victim's autopsy becomes very important. The autopsy documentation for this case has been a disaster. Wound descriptions have been moved and relocated, notes taken during the autopsy have been burned and rewritten, independent recollection has differed from the official record, and so on. Had the wounds been thoroughly analyzed right after the event in Dallas for exact entry and exit points together with collecting any bullet slug materials, our understanding of true possible sniper locations would have been greatly improved. Instead, we have evidence that wound locations were relocated at Bethesda, and surgery was done on the body, prior to the autopsy. For example, the neck wound was initially a small circular wound that later became a long gash. The back of the head was reported to have a wound the size of a baseball. However, later autopsy pictures were showing the back of the head fully intact. Once the autopsy was completed, all the participants were required to sign a contract to maintain absolute confidentiality. Recently, a more detailed autopsy description has been disclosed (4.2).

The information that would be presented by the Warren Commission would eventually be selective and tailored to support the lone nut theory. Certain witnesses would be disregarded or all together ignored. When tests would be conducted, the participants would only be the ones that supported the desired narrative. For example, several timing tests were run to see if Marion Baker and Lee Harvey Oswald could meet in the lunch room with Lee starting on the sixth floor and Marion starting on his motorcycle. Marion would pretend to hear the shots, race up to the TSBD, join up with Mr. Truly, check the elevators, and finally move to the stairs. The Oswald component of this test would include a start on the sixth floor, hide the weapon, run to the stairs, and head down to the second floor. These tests are responsible for deriving the 90 second duration. Unfortunately, the two girls (Victoria Adams and Sandra Styles) were never included in the time trials. Why? Remember, they never observed or heard Oswald anywhere on the stairs. The stairs were wooden and must have created noise when walking on them. Why not try and nail down the two girls' movements with those of Marion Baker and Roy Truly? Why not do a complete thorough job of this critical timing?

What is worse, several of the witnesses started to become scared to speak up. The fear to them and their families was real and directly tied to the mysterious deaths that started to occur. Victoria Adams became very concerned for her personal safety and had to leave Dallas. She felt her testimony was altered and not properly accepted to the point she started to fear the worst.

SUMMARY and CONCLUSIONS

1) Three shells were found on the floor in the TSBD sixth floor sniper's nest. If the rifle had a cartridge in the chamber ready to fire, and three shots were then fired, there would only need to be two shells ejected. The third shell would not need to be ejected, especially when the assassin is likely in a hurry to get out of the sniper's nest. When the weapon was found, a new cartridge was indeed in the chamber.

2) The head shot caused a motion from front to rear due to an entry from the front.

3) The bullet that hit John Connally is not the same bullet that JFK is reacting to in Z224. The time difference between shots is 1.32 seconds.

4) The head shot at Z313 occurred 4.9 seconds after Z224. For the three shots discussed in this chapter, the time before the first and second shot is 1.32 seconds and the time between shot two and three is 4.9 seconds.

5) The angle of entry at Z200 is too steep to line up with John Connally's wound entry point.

6) Projecting angles from inside the limousine is not reliable with the data we

have. A small movement in the limousine could very easily move the line of sight to one of the other tall buildings or locations within Dealey Plaza.

7) In this chapter, we discussed the JFK head wound, JFK's reaction to a bullet wound in either his neck or back, and the John Connally's wound originating in his back. We have no information about the timing of additional shots that possibly hit Connally or the time in the sequence when James Tague was wounded.

Chapter 6 – Aftermath in Dealey Plaza and Other Important Testimony

As I stated in several parts of this text, the story of the JFK assassination is a complex story with a lot of sub topics. In this chapter, I will discuss some of the other events that occurred in the direct aftermath of the assassination. In addition, this chapter will look at some of the other key testimony that needs to be considered when researching the assassination. I always regarded these details as important. In many cases, conclusions cannot be drawn with any kind of certainty, but nevertheless, they need to be considered.

Dealey Plaza Testimony

During the assassination, there were many people on the ground level and in the various buildings. The amount of testimony that they gave would be sifted through for several years. Many of them reported hearing three shots with some hearing more. The location of the shots varied between higher up in the buildings to ground level around the triple underpass area. As can be expected, it is difficult to get consistency with ear witness testimony. Because of the excitement of seeing a presidential motorcade together with unexpected gun fire, we can understand the sound registration would be inconsistent. Even so, there are some consistencies that comes thru in the testimony.

In listening to the witnesses' interviews and reading their testimony, the one strange thing that has been repeated by several of them is the timing of the shots. In chapter 5, three of the shots were examined in detail. Based on a close look at the Zapruder frames, we can estimate the time between the shots as 1.32 seconds and 4.9 seconds. This is completely opposite to what these witnesses have reported. Most witnesses have reported the longer pause to be between shots 1 and 2, and a very short time between 2 and 3. Their description in many cases indicates 2 and 3 to be almost on top of one another.

Lee bowers, the witness from the train tower behind the picket fence, reported a very quick succession for a total of three shots in about two seconds, with 2 and 3 almost on top of one another. Malcolm Summers, the witness near the south edge of Elm Street who was met with someone holding a gun, heard the shots within about 5 second. He indicated a long pause (four seconds) between 1 and 2, and one second between 2 and 3. The characteristic of a long pause and then quick succession is consistent among many other witnesses who heard the shots. This is one of the stranger reports from the witnesses. Looking at the Zapruder film, it appears JFK and Connally have been hit, then there is a long pause, and then the head shot. Maybe the shot just before the head shot is the one responsible for James Tague's wound.

Harold Norman (6.1) worked in the TSBD and was a coworker of Lee Harvey Oswald. He was also well known amongst several of the other employees. During the assassination, Norman and two other coworkers (James Jarman and Bonnie Ray Williams) were seated in the fifth floor directly below the sniper's nest on the sixth floor. Harold Norman's testimony is that he could hear the rifle shooting along with the ratcheting of the bolt action between shots. He also testified that he heard three shells hit the floor above him in between each of the first two shots and after the third. His testimony indicates a fourth cartridge was loaded after the third shell was ejected. Jarman and Williams never did confirm the same sounds that Harold Norman reported. If fact, both indicated the second and third shots were very close together which does not leave time to actuate the bolt action. These three witnesses are seated side by side and they heard different sequences. None of the three ever heard any footsteps above them as if someone was running to the stairway.

Prior to the shots fired, Bonnie Ray Williams (6.2) ate his lunch on the sixth floor. He was up there between 12:00 and 12:10 or 12:15. He left behind a lunch sack, chicken bones and an empty Dr. Pepper bottle. Later, he confirmed he was up there during that time. Right after he finished his lunch, he went down one flight to the fifth floor to meet up with Harold Norman and James Jarman.

While he was on the sixth floor, Bonnie Ray Williams did not hear anyone else walking or moving around. He never saw Oswald at any time. As noted early, the upper floors of the TSBD are one continuous area with boxes of books stacked. It is strange that if Oswald was planning to fire the weapon, from the sixth floor, why was he not seen or heard at all by Bonnie Ray Williams? The presidential motorcade was planning to arrive in Dealey Plaza at 12:15. It arrived at 12:30 running 15 minutes late. Bonnie Ray never heard or seen anyone else in this area. Furthermore, Bonnie Ray could hear his coworkers rustling around on the fifth floor below.

Additional critical witnesses were located on the top of the triple underpass. This area is part of the railroad tracks that were present along the outer edge of Dealey Plaza. From this location, the witnesses could see the motorcade approaching after making the sharp turn onto Elm Street. Three witnesses, James Simmons, Richard Dodd, and Sam Holland were there. Their testimony includes seeing puffs of smoke linger around the grassy knoll picket fence. Smoke after the shots could have been from someone firing a weapon. They went back to that area and found fresh muddy foot prints. Remember, that earlier that morning, it had rained in Dallas. Fresh foot prints had to have been developed after the morning rain. From their vantage point, on top of the triple underpass, these witnesses heard four shots.

Ed Hoffman

Ed Hoffman (6.3) witnessed activities behind the picket fence from a Stemmons Freeway ramp. As you recall, the motorcade was going down Elm Street in order to get on to the Stemmons freeway. Hoffman decided to watch the motorcade downstream from Dealey Plaza as it got onto the freeway. This was a last minute decision since he had left work early for a tooth issue. His view of the motorcade would allow him to see inside the limousine from above. While it was approaching, he saw two men behind the picket fence, break down a rifle, and then walk in different directions. As the limousine proceeded, he could see the aftermath inside from above.

Hoffman was deaf and had no testimony about the shots fired. But his viewing angle was unique and provided some collaboration of Lee Bowers testimony.

Buell Wesley Frazier

One of the most important people in this story is Buell Wesley Frazier (6.4). At the time of the assassination, he was 19 years old and had been working at the TSBD for just a few months. He is indirectly responsible for Lee Harvey Oswald submitting the job application at TSBD. He will be referred to as Wes here, since that is what he went by back then. Wes lived in Irving with his sister, Linnie May Randle, and her husband. Her house was just down the block from Ruth Paine. Mrs. Paine is the person who took in Lee Oswald, Marina, and their children during the time before the assassination. In conversation between Ruth Paine and Wes's sister, Mrs. Paine mentioned that Lee had been out of work. When the word got back to Wes, he asked at the TSBD to see if they were still taking applications. Following this question from Wes, Lee would fill out an application. Within a short time, Lee had begun work there and Wes was his primary mentor. Oswald would quickly learn the requirements of Wes's job and would help to pull and fill book orders.

Wes found Lee quiet and easy to work with. Since Wes and Lee lived so close together, Wes offered to take Lee back and forth to work. Oswald did not have a car or driver's license and Wes did own a car. Lee had taken residency in a boarding house in Oak Cliff and said he would stay close to the TSBD during the week, but would like to head back to Irving with Wes on weekends.

This pattern continued until on Thursday November 21, 1963, Lee Oswald asked Wes if he could have a ride back to Irving that night. Wes told him yes, but then later asked Lee why tonight, tonight is Thursday? Lee explained that he needed to pick up some curtain rods at the house in Irving for his apartment down in Oak

Cliff. The next morning, Lee arrived at Wes's sister house with the package and waited for Wes to finish breakfast. Lee put the package in the back seat of Wes's car. When the two arrived at the TSBD, Lee grabbed the package and walked into the building.

Following the assassination, the Dallas Police and then the Warren Commission hammered Wes with questions about his relation with Lee and the details of the package. At one point, Wes was placed under arrest in order to ask additional questions. Later on, both Wes's sister and Wes had been required to give formal testimony to the Warren Commission. For the Warren Commission, they were obviously trying to establish the package contained the Manlicher Carcano rifle that was found on the sixth floor and was later established as being purchased by Oswald. The problem became the size of the package.

Thru their testimony, Linnie May estimated a length of 27 inches and a width "span of a hand" of 6-7 inches and Wes estimated 24 inches (give or take two inches), with a width of 5-6 inches. No comments were made about the thickness of the package. Oswald walked over to the Randle's house on Friday morning in order to join Wes for his ride to work. Linnie May was at the kitchen sink when she saw Oswald walking with the package. She saw Oswald carrying it in his hand alongside his body. He was holding the top of the package and it did not touch the ground. Carrying the package like this does indicate a length of under 27 inches. Also, carrying from the top and letting it hang downward like this points to a lighter weight than a rifle of this size.

Figure 6.1 – Manlicher Carcano Rifle Dimensions – *courtesy of the National Archives CE139*

Figure 6.1 shows the rifle in a broken down condition. This is typically what is done to transport the weapon. The lower half with the wooden stock and support has a length of 35 inches with a width that is within 5-6 inches. The upper half has a length of approximately 28 inches with the width within 5-6 inches. With the weapon assembled, the length is 40 inches and the width is 10-12 inches. The weight of the rifle is estimated at 7.5 pounds.

In Wes's testimony, he noted that Lee had put the package in the back seat on the passenger's side of the car. This happened while Lee was waiting outside and Wes was getting ready for work. When Wes got into the driver's side of the car, he glanced over his shoulder and saw the package. He asked Lee what it was, and Lee reminded him that it was the curtain rods he came back for. Wes said the package was on Lee's side of the car (passenger) and it extended to the center of the seat. The back seat of the car Wes was driving is estimated to be 48.8 inches. This is taken from the 1953 user's manual. Based on the bench length of the back seat at 48.8 inches, the center of the seat would be 24.4 inches. The overall average width of this vehicle is about 74 inches. Back then, the depth of the inner and outer doors was much wider than what we have today. Each side is close to 12 inches. This checks out with a bench width or near 50 inches.

Several years later, Wes had an opportunity to see the Manlicher Carcano rifle up close. This was a duplicate to the one Oswald had owned. Wes unequivocally stated there is no way that rifle was broken down and placed in the package he saw that morning. He made this statement several times over the years.

Initial Evidence and More Witness Testimony

Roger Craig (6.5) was a plan clothes Dallas detective who quickly ran to Dealey Plaza after hearing the shots. He was positioned a block away and was only there to watch the motorcade go by. Upon hearing the shots, he immediately ran across the middle grass area to Dealey Plaza. When he arrived at Elm Street, he saw a police officer running up the hill. He assumed this man had information about the origin of the shots, so Craig followed him. By the time he had reached the fence, several police officers and bystanders had arrived in this immediate area. In his testimony and interviews, he presents a different method of escape for Oswald than what was previously noted. According to Craig, a man, later identified as Oswald, ran down the Grassy Knoll area and jumped into a green colored Rambler station wagon. This vehicle description matches Ruth Paine's vehicle at that time. Craig would later meet Oswald as he was being questioned at police headquarters. He immediately recognized him as the man who jumped in the Rambler.

Very soon after checking areas around the picket fence, Roger Craig would join other officers in the sixth floor of the TSBD. According to Roger Craig, he was right there when the weapon was found. He describes a similar, but different ammunition size weapon than the Manlicher Carcano rifle. According to Craig's observations, the barrel of the rife was stamped with the designation "7.65 mm Mauser". The different size means the shells that were found in the sniper's nest are not compatible with the rifle that was just found. One of the deputies that was present during this time was Seymour Weitzman (6.6). He made the first official affidavit that the weapon found was a German Mauser which has a 7.65 mm caliber. This means the diameter of the bullet and internal diameter of the gun barrel are nominally 7.65 mm. Seymour was regarded as very knowledgeable with rifles since he owned a rifle shop in town. This initial designation became a huge problem for the evidence. The shells found in the sniper's nest were 6.5 mm caliber which means they did not come from this weapon. Later, Seymour Weitzman would try to explain this as an initial error since the two weapons are similar.

I encourage you to view the interviews of both these witnesses. The fact that the rifle had a different caliber than the shells, and the rifle was stamped with the make and caliber is a big problem for the evidence in this case. Documenting the caliber in an affidavit usually means the author is sure about what he just saw. Why it later changed is one of the many mysteries in this case.

The Three Tramps / Jim Braden

Several people were apprehended and questioned shortly after the assassination. It appears the scene was very chaotic with the police and detectives trying to get as much evidence and information as quickly as possible. The crime scene was not locked down, so people could come and go at will. I think if this event happened today, this entire area would have immediately been locked down to prevent people from leaving and entering. From all the accounts, during the time just after the assassination, people were free to enter and leave Dealey Plaza, also areas near Parkland hospital where the limousine was parked, and the Dallas police station. One of the films taken of the detectives and police gathering evidence on the sixth floor was from a camera crew and reporter. They had snuck in as the police were working. To preserve the film, the reporter pulled it from the camera and tossed it out the window to one of his colleagues standing below. With these events happening around and the nature of a compromised crime scene, the chain of evidence for this case has always been in question.

Three men would be removed from one of the train cars behind the parking area just north of the picket fence. Recall that a branch of train tracks, with train cars, were located in this area along the perimeter. These men would later be listed as "the three tramps". Evidence did not indicate any foul play; however, their attire raised some eyebrows. It appears that they are neat and clean for people that are described as hobos. There are several pictures of the tramps on line and may even be captured in a video.

Probably one of the more mysterious characters apprehended in Dealey Plaza was Eugene Hale Brading (known as Jim Braden). Braden had a long criminal record of 35 arrests for burglary, bookmaking, and embezzlement. He was found in the Dal Tex Building which is just east of TSBD. He claimed he was only there to make a phone call. After his apprehension and questioning, he was later released. Braden was later linked to Jack Ruby and other Mafia personnel. There was never any definite link established between Braden and the assassination. However, his background does raise concerns. Anytime a person with a previous criminal record is near the occurrence of a new crime, the police do get concerned. He was in the Dal Tex building while the shots were fired.

SUMMARY and CONCLUSIONS

1) The mysterious figure in Dealey Plaza has not been identified. It is inconclusive whether or not this is a person walking away.

2) The ear witness testimony in general reports a longer pause between shots 1 and 2 and a short pause between 2 and 3. My conclusion is that some of the shots were fired on top of one another creating a single sound to the witnesses. I am confident 5 or more shots were fired.

3) Harold Norman's testimony is that he heard three shots in even succession directly above his position on the fifth floor. He could hear the ratcheting of the

bolt action and the shells hitting the floor. The two other witnesses next to him did not hear this. These two men both reported a long pause between shots one and two, and two and three very close together, whereas Harold Norman reported evenly spaced shots.

4) The activity on the fifth and sixth floors of the TSBD places employees around the sniper's nest with no one seeing Oswald in the time frame of 12:00 to 12:30.

5) The package that Lee Oswald brought to the TSBD on November 22, 1963, was too short to carry the wooden stock portion of the Manlicher Carcano rifle. It may have contained the upper portion of the weapon.

6) The initial official weapon description was a 7.65 mm German Mauser. Later this was changed to a 6.5 mm Manlicher Carcano. The shells found in the sniper's nest are for a 6.5 mm caliber weapon.

7) The alleged crime scene on the sixth floor of the TSBD was not sealed. This did not preserve the chain of evidence. Had this case gone to trial, this fact could have produced reasonable doubt.

Chapter 7 – Additional Oswald Details

As noted in the previous chapters, there is a lot of mystery surrounding Oswald. He had joined the Marines at an early age and had assignments that included one in Atsugi Japan in 1957. Later, he would defect to Russia (1959-1962) and became married to Marina. This was a strange thing to do since most people were trying to defect from Russia to America. While in Russia, he attempted suicide.

When he came back to America, it is confusing to understand what exactly he was doing and who were his associations. He may have been part of the CIA or FBI, or possibly both. In all my research, I was amazed how many people were associated with the Central Intelligence Agency (CIA). It seems the CIA utilized random people of various backgrounds for a wide range of tasks. I believe that trying to solve some of these mysteries requires one to "follow the money". If Oswald was part of the CIA, did they pay him? Did the CIA pay any of the contacts they utilized?

James Hosty was an FBI agent who was responsible for investigating Oswald. It is not clear if he was getting information from Oswald or he was simply there to keep an eye on Oswald. Prior to the assassination, Hosty visited Marina Oswald and asked her some questions. When Lee Oswald became aware of this, he went to the local FBI office to confront Hosty. Hosty was not available and Oswald ended up leaving a note for Hosty. Later, this note was destroyed just after Oswald was killed. Hosty later said the note was from Oswald telling him to basically "leave his wife alone".

Very mysterious is Oswald's trip to New Orleans and Mexico City. These occurred shortly before the assassination. I have always been confused about the timing of these trips and more importantly, who and how were they financed. Oswald allegedly made several visits to the US Embassy while he was in Mexico City. As noted early on in the text, the embassy photo surveillance captured pictures of someone who is not the Oswald we know (figure 7.1). In fact, some testimony places Oswald in Dallas during this same time frame (7.1).

Comm. Exh. 237

Figure 7.1 – Second Oswald at the Mexico Embassy – *courtesy of the National Archives CE237*

One of the more famous pieces of information that came about during this time frame is the backyard photo. This photo created a lot of concern since it showed Oswald with the Manlicher Carcano rifle and his revolver all in one photo. Marina Oswald stated that she took this photo at Lee's request.

Figure 7.2 Backyard photo of Oswald with his weapons and a Marxist newspaper -*courtesy of the National Archives CE134*

Much analysis of this photo has been done in order to prove it is real and not a fake. Oswald had stated when he was in police custody in Dallas that this picture was a fake.

On April 10, 1963 (several months before the JFK assassination), Major General Edwin Walker was the target of an attempted assassination. Later, it would be presented that this assassination attempt was done by Lee Oswald using his rifle. The location for this was

80

at Walker's home in Dallas Texas. Assuming this was indeed done by Oswald, several questions arise.

1) How did Oswald transport the rifle? He did not drive or own a car.

2) Did someone help him with this attempt?

3) If he later would be the shooter in Dealey Plaza, how did he hit that target but missed this target from less than 30 feet away, and it was not moving?

4) Did he do this as a warning sign and not an actual assassination attempt?

Just after the assassination, while Oswald was in Dallas police custody, a paraffin test was run. This test is used to determine if a person recently fired a weapon. The way this is done is to use warm paraffin wax and apply it to the skin. When the wax hardens, it draws out the possible nitrates that are on the skin. If a weapon has recently been fired, the skin should contain nitrates. This test was performed on Oswald's cheek and hands. The results indicated that Oswald had nitrates on his hands and not his cheek. He would most definitely show the residue on his check if he recently fired a rifle. The test was done several ways and still showed negative for his right cheek. However, his hands did indicate some nitrates which may have been from the boxes he handled in the TSBD. This type of evidence does lean towards reasonable doubt and must be considered when discussing Oswald's guilt or innocence.

After the assassination, Oswald left the TSBD and Dealey Plaza and made a brief stop at his boarding house in Oak Cliff. Earlene Roberts, the caretaker for this house, testified that Oswald arrived at 1 pm and briefly grabbed a jacket and left. He was registered as O. H. Lee at this home. Once he left, thru the front door, he went out the corner and appeared to be waiting for a bus. The time of the Tippit shooting was estimated to be about 1:15. Back at the TSBD, a rollcall was being conducted at this same time. Oswald was the only missing employee. Oswald would shortly be apprehended in a nearby theater.

These fast moving events occurred right after the assassination. The timeline shows within one hour beginning at 12:30, shots were fired in Dealey Plaza, Oswald left the scene grabbed a bus, then grabbed a cab, and arrived at the boarding house at 1 pm. About 1:15, officer Tippit is shot. At 1:50, Oswald is apprehended in the Texas theater. Oswald was definitely acting strange. Whether this was him running from the scene as the assassin, or he sensed he was somehow being framed as a patsy is not known.

Oswald spent Friday afternoon thru Sunday morning in custody at the Dallas local police station. Recall that as he was being moved on Sunday morning, Jack Ruby came in and shot him. While Oswald was in his jail cell, he requested to make a phone call. This occurred late Saturday evening (7.2). The story surrounding this call is extremely bizarre. Oswald was trying to call Raleigh North Carolina to reach a man named John Hurt. To do this, the call would have to be placed as "collect". That means the person who would receive the call needs to acknowledge that he or she will pay for this call. Furthermore, calls from the Dallas Police station jail needed to go thru their main switchboard that included phone operators. This procedure required the operators located in the switchboard room to call the number, establish if calling collect was acceptable, and then patch the requesting party into the call. Two men in dark suits arrived once it was known that Oswald was going to request this call. When the call was attempted (by Oswald) the dark suit men requested that the operator inform Oswald that the party in Raleigh did not pick up the call. How this transpired is; Oswald called into the switchboard with the name and number, Oswald is put on hold, and then shortly after, the operator was told to say no one answered, even though she never attempted the call.

The person Oswald was trying to reach was John D. Hurt. He had been a special agent of the US army counter intelligence division. By the time Oswald was trying to reach him, he had since retired from counter intelligence and his personal health was failing. His health issues were severe and he was regarded as disabled.

He had several physical and phycological medical issues. It was later suggested that the John Hurt character was acting as an intelligence cutout. This type of procedure is typically used when a person is on a dangerous intelligence mission. The leader making the assignment will direct the person to call a third party if they get into trouble. This is used so that the leader cannot be tied to the details of a critical mission. The third party is considered an intelligence cutout so that no communication can get back to the original intelligence source. Oswald was likely attempting this call based on instructions from above. Unfortunately, the John Hurt character had no real function at the time and was more of a fake cutout, than someone who could help Oswald. It appears someone gave Oswald the information to send him down a dead end path.

The entire story of Lee Harvey Oswald is complex and mysterious. A lot of the details we have are incomplete and circumstantial. The details point to someone who was constantly searching for something, but that he never quite gets to where he Is trying to go. Many times, his goals appear to be completely 180 degrees apposite of one another. While in New Orleans he was associated with a group that appeared to be resistance against Cuba, but then he was later found to be fighting for "hands off Cuba". If we could somehow know more about what he was doing in 1963, we might have a better understanding of his role in this entire event.

SUMMARY and CONCLUSIONS

1) It is not clear what if any association Oswald had with the CIA or FBI other than being watched by James Hosty of the FBI.

2) After the assassination, the paraffin test done on Oswald did not indicate he recently fired a rifle. After the assassination, Oswald had no time to remove nitrates from hi cheek area.

3) Oswald's attempted call to John Hurt is strange. It is not clear who gave Oswald this contact.

Epilogue

The preceding chapters of the text present some of the most important facts and details that surrounded the JFK assassination on November 22, 1963. And there is so much more. The branches of this story are puzzling and in many cases incapable of reaching a conclusion with any kind of specificity. I tried to focus on the most pertinent facts that can be discussed with some semblance of completion, and which are most applicable to reach an understanding of the event.

From all my research into this event, I have concluded that more than one person was involved with this assassination. The role, if any, by Lee Harvey Oswald I just cannot define. There is some evidence that points to guilt and some evidence the points to innocence. Other evidence is confusing, cannot be confirmed, and appears to be in an unrelated direction.

Putting all this together, I just cannot imagine anyone shooting from the sixth floor of the TSBD. It sounds like during the course of their daily work assignments, the employees who were pulling and filling the book orders would traverse the floors using the elevators and stairs popping in and out of each floor. It just does not seem probable for someone to sit in the corner and assemble a rifle and then start firing, and expect to go unnoticed. People were all around that area just prior to the assassination. No one could ever go totally unnoticed. Police officers quickly responded and other employees were on the stairway. If Oswald did this shooting, he was very fortunate to not be positively seen in the act, or at least getting prepared for the shooting. The way he left the scene, either by bus or someone picked him up, he definitely wanted to get away from that area. One witness, Howard Brennan, witnessed the assassination directly across the street from the TSBD. He testified he saw a man with a weapon, but could not later identify him as Oswald. I think the following additional conclusions are critical to this study. But with some of these items, we have additional questions.

Single Bullet Theory does not hold up

I think the evidence clearly does not support the Single Bullet Theory. This theory is necessary for the assassination to take place in 6 seconds, from a single assassin, using the Manlicher Carcano rifle, and result in the wounds to JFK, John Connally, and James Tague. If this theory is not fact, then the premise of a lone nut assassin falls apart. Bottom line, the Single Bullet Theory could not have taken place. As compelling as the argument is from Dr. Cyril Wecht about the condition of the bullet found at Parkland, I think there is a single frame of the Zapruder film that is also just as compelling. Frame Z224 shows the bullet flipping John

Connally's lapel over at the same time JFK and Jackie are reacting to the previous shot. It is impossible to be from the same bullet. Couple this with the testimony of Nellie Connally and this indeed requires two separate shots. Without these wounds caused by a single bullet and without moving the back wound to the throat wound location, we cannot meet the Warren Commission's theory of the event.

This leads to another question which is, how did the bullet from the Manlicher Carcano rifle show up in Parkland hospital. Did it fall out of one of the wounds or was it planted by a conspirator? The back wound on JFK did not enter into the lung cavity. Could the bullet have been there while he was being tended to in the emergency room? Could trying to revive him actually push this bullet out of his back? Or did someone plant it?

Jack Ruby gunned down Oswald a few days later in the basement of the police station. Ruby was well known around Dallas. He owned and managed the Carousal nightclub. Several of his acquaintances were Dallas police officers. His background had some ties to organized crime. Ruby was observed at Parkland hospital on Friday and also the Dallas police station. Ruby is captured in several photos over the weekend at both Parkland Hospital and the police station. He was posing as a newspaper reporter with a pad and pen in his hand. His club was shut down over the weekend and he seemed to be closely following the assassination developments. Could he have planted the bullet? Was he going to try and shoot Oswald at the police station sooner than he did? Answers to these questions were never found.

Head Shot from the Front

This has been debated and analyzed. I do not see how this shot can enter from the rear. Without the shot originating from behind, multiple shooters are involved. The film evidence and Parkland hospital medical staff point to this shot originating from the front of JFK. Evidence of people on the knoll indicates this as a likely spot. In addition to the film evidence and the momentum analysis, I think an additional key fact tells me something or someone behind the fence was being protected. The fact that at least two men were preventing people from entering is a significant occurrence. One of people who was restricted from this area was a Dallas police officer.

Patsy

If a conspiracy existed, was Oswald indeed slated to be the patsy? Was he going to be the fall guy? It appears that Oswald was somehow aware of what was happening and that he was possibly intended to be the main suspect. Had he been as surprised about the events as much as everyone else in Dealey Plaza and the TSBD, he would have likely stayed around. The fact that he left the scene abruptly makes you think he knew something more. This leads to a very important question from this point of view. If the conspirators expected to pin it on Oswald, how did they keep him out of sight during the exact time shots were fired? Several people saw him around the second floor just before the motorcade arrived. No one reported seeing him on the sixth or fifth floor after 12 pm. How did they keep him out of sight on the second floor? The answer may have been a pre-arranged phone call from someone to Oswald.

It was common practice back then for people to use random pay phones for receiving phone calls. Did Oswald give out a number for someone to reach him at this time? If true, he was likely told to be there to receive a call at 12:15 to 12:30. As the motorcade approached Dealey Plaza, the call was then made. But with this strategy, the conspirators have to be sure nobody stayed behind in the lunchroom or near the closest pay phone. All it would have taken is one other person to be there in the lunchroom, at that exact time, to give Oswald a finite alibi. Was the strategy to at least pin the weapon on Oswald and then with him soon to be silenced, it would not matter whether or not he pulled the trigger? When you try to reason this out, it seems creating a true patsy is difficult and may require back up plans with possible alternate candidates.

Maybe the back up patsy was Jim Braden. Very little information about his movements in Dealey Plaza is available. He was apprehended and then quickly released. Being in the Dal Tex Building during the time shots were fired, makes him a candidate for this roll.

Oswald's Irving Package

On Friday morning, Oswald went to work with Wes Frazier and brought in a brown paper wrapped package. Oswald told Wes it was curtain rods for his Oak Cliff apartment. After the assassination, it was determined that the curtains Oswald had in his apartment were adequate and working fine. What was in this package? I think we can be very sure it was not the entire Manlicher Carcano rifle. It could have been the top half of the rifle, but then how did the lower half get there? How did Oswald normally transport his rifle, to go to the shooting range?

When using a rifle with a scope, recalibration is required. The scope can easily be knock out of calibration when the weapon is transported. A single bump can throw this alignment off. The calibration procedure requires using a special target for determining the amount of offset required. The adjustments of the scope typically include an up and down (vertical) adjustment and a left and right adjustment. When the weapon is separated, or broken down, the scope calibration may get thrown off.

This to me is one of many key open issues of the case. If he was the lone assassin and if he brought the rifle to the TSBD on the day of the assassination, he would have likely made the assassination decision sometime on Thursday. This would have been prior to telling Wes he wanted to go back to Irving that night. After the assassination, the police went to Ruth Paine's house and asked Marina Oswald if her husband had a weapon. Marina brought the police into the garage and showed them a rolled up blanket. When they picked it up, nothing was in the blanket. Ruth Paine was shocked because she did not know a weapon had been stored in her garage. There has got to be more to this part of the story. Allowing for just 24 hours of planning is just not enough. What was in the package? If not part of a rifle, what was wrapped in the package?

Summary

In summary, this case is complex and still has many open ends. The subjects discussed in this text are only a handful of the details of a story that has only diverged over time. I tried to focus on the most relevant items in an effort to both inform the reader and also present areas of closure were possible.

A defining point where this case started to get away was when the body was removed from Dallas. All control was lost and it appears that the evidence was altered. Very shortly after the assassination, one of the principal researchers documented the issues with the autopsy and body evidence (4.1). Had these events not happened, I think everyone would have a clear picture of direction of fire, number of wounds, etc.

The picture that was being painted by the Warren Commission was predetermined rather than one of true inquiry. As you read thru the depositions of the witnesses, you can clearly see what path the commission is on and what their charter is. It needs to be noted that the commission was different from a true legal case that includes discovery and cross examination. In their mind, the person guilty of this crime acted alone. Now that he is deceased, there would be no actual trial.

As part of my job responsibilities, I get involved in expert witness support and testimony. I have had to give several depositions over the years. The questioning is always direct with an effort to fully document important technical data and opinions. I do not see the same effort in the Warren Commission testimony. For example, why could it not be absolutely established whether or not Oswald had a coke in his hand when he was stopped at the second floor lunchroom of the TSBD. This is one example of many.

My opinion is that multiple people were involved. Oswald had to be aware of this plot in some form, but I really doubt if he was a shooter. I think the pieces that had to fall in place for him not be caught red handed are too much of an unrealistic probability. Whether or not he was intended to be the fall guy (or patsy) by the planners is an open question. I think this conclusion is shared by most serious researchers. The question of who was part of the "multiple people" gets to be more complicated. At this point in the story, we can still only speculate with hope that someday we can learn more.

Reference Books and Films

There is an abundant amount of evidence and information available that pertains to the JFK Assassination. In addition to many publications, there is many pictures online and testimony in the form of written depositions and YOUTUBE videos. Many of the videos include detailed interviews of key witnesses like Lee Bowers, John Connally, Nellie Connally, TSBD employees, eye witnesses in Dealey Plaza, and more. Over the many years of my research, I particularly found the interviews of witnesses just after the assassination very helpful. The following references are my suggestions for key evidence and my recommended primary sources. I used these references throughout my text.

1.1 Marion Baker Testimony

1.2 The Girl on the Stairs – by Barry Ernest

1.3 Joe M. Smith Testimony

1.4 Malcolm Summers Testimony

2.1 A Rose by Many Other Names – by Todd C. Elliott

2.2 The Man who Knew Too Much – by Dick Russell

2.3 Hit List – by Richard Belzer

2.4 Executive Action (1973 film)

4.1 Best Evidence – by David Lifton

4.2 At the Cold Shoulder of History – by James C. Jenkins

4.3 John Connally Interviews and Testimony

4.4 Zapruder Film

5.1 Mary Moorman photo

5.2 Enemy of the Truth – by Sherry P. Fiester

5.3 Nellie Connally Interviews and Testimony

6.1 Harold Norman Interviews and Testimony

6.2 Bonnie Ray Williams Interviews and Testimony

6.3 Ed Hoffman Interviews and Testimony

6.4 Buell Wesley Fraizer Interviews and Testimony

6.5 Roger Craig Interviews and Testimony

6.6 Seymour Weitzman Testimony

7.1 Silvia Odio Testimony

7.2 Dr Grover Proctor's Presentation about Oswald's Call to Raleigh

About the Author

Anthony Rante was born in Chicago Illinois. During his education, he gravitated towards the sciences like mathematics and physics. He obtained a Bachelor's in Mechanical Engineering in 1979. During his career, he has held various Engineering positions and has been part of several publications. He currently is President and Principal Engineer for Artech Engineering.

Anthony's dedication to the field of Engineering shines thru in this review of the assassination. He uses his Engineering knowledge and crime details, together with the existing evidence, to help the reader learn about this event. The text includes pictures and diagrams along with references to current additional sources of information. The analytical approach of this study is intended to both describe the historical events and also present a technical understanding of what transpired. Whether you are familiar with this event or are new to it, the text will help you understand the details of the story and become acquainted with this unique cast of characters.